GROUP MEMBER

LIVING OUT THE PERSPECTIVE-CHANGING
PARABLES JESUS TOLD

inVerted

TOM ELLSWORTH

NANCY KARPENSKE

Standard®
PUBLISHING

Cincinnati, Ohio

Published by Standard Publishing, Cincinnati, Ohio
www.standardpub.com

Copyright © 2011 by Standard Publishing

Also available: *Inverted*, ISBN 978-0-7847-2925-0, copyright © 2011 by Standard Publishing

Printed in: United States of America
Acquisitions editor: Dale Reeves
Project editor: Laura Derico
Cover design: Thinkpen Design Inc., www.thinkpendesign.com
Interior design: Dina Sorn at Ahaa! Design

ISBN 978-0-7847-2926-7

16 15 14 13 12 11   1 2 3 4 5 6 7 8 9

Contents

How to Use This Guide 4

SESSION 1   Be Grateful 7
The parable of the whiny workers
Matthew 20:1-16

SESSION 2   Be Compassionate 14
The parable of the roadside rescue
Luke 10:25-37

SESSION 3   Be Forgiving 21
The parable of the shocking servant
Matthew 18:21-35

SESSION 4   Be Gracious 28
The parable of the warmest welcome
Luke 15:11-32

SESSION 5   Be Faithful 35
The parable of the master's money
Luke 19:12-26

SESSION 6   Be Authentic 42
The parable of the pompous and pious prayers
Luke 18:9-14

SESSION 7   Be Perceptive 50
The parable of the street-smart steward
Luke 16:1-13

SESSION 8   Be Vigilant 57
The parable of the bewildered bridesmaids
Matthew 25:1-13

How to Use This Guide

This guide is designed for small group use with the companion book, *Inverted*. It will help your group discuss the ideas from *Inverted* and apply them in your lives. This happens best in groups that are growing together in real friendships, real faith, and real fun!

TRUE TO THE BIBLE

The aim is not to study a book however. It is to study God's Word, using *Inverted* as a launching pad. We have designed this guide, like all the Standard Publishing products you've come to trust, to be true to the Bible.

TRUE TO LIFE

We designed this guide also to be true to life—life in the real world of friends, spouses, disappointments, kids, jobs, bills, and other everyday circumstances. We want this guide to help your faith intersect with other aspects of your life so you will live the life that Jesus promised: life to the full!

A number of features make this guide distinctive:

> *It is designed for busy people.* You will not need to spend hours preparing for meetings, whether you are the leader or another member of the group. However, reading the companion book, *Inverted*, is highly recommended to help you get the most out of this study.

> *It is designed for people at various maturity levels.* You do not need to be a Bible scholar to facilitate or participate in these studies. The companion book will provide the teaching for each session. Your job is to discuss the truths from God's Word and apply them to your life.

> *It is designed to develop community.* Your group—whether you are a Sunday school class, Bible study, or small group—will grow closer to one another as you share your stories, study the Word, and serve together. The optimal number of participants in a group is usually about three to ten, depending on a variety of circumstances. But larger groups can still be very effective. We suggest you subgroup if your group is larger than twelve. You may want to break into several groups of three to six during the Study and Apply sections, for instance, for deeper discussion and more authentic application.

> *It is designed to help you grow spiritually.* Real, lasting life change is the primary goal. The Holy Spirit will transform you as you allow him to work through God's Word and other group members to encourage, support, admonish, and pray for one another. Your group will employ Colossians 3:16: "Let the word of Christ dwell in you richly as you teach and admonish one another with all wisdom."

HOW EACH SESSION IS ORGANIZED

Leader Preparation: This section is designed to prepare the leader's heart and mind for the meeting. To maximize opportunities for spiritual growth in your group, take time to read and reflect. Also use this time to pray for group members.

Bible Study Agenda: This study is designed to help participants *discover* truth from God's Word through group interaction rather than having the leader just *tell* them what it says. Participants will observe, contemplate, wrestle with, and take action on Scripture. Use the questions to facilitate lively interaction among group members. This will lead people to aha moments—when they *get it.* Ask follow-up questions to keep a good discussion moving. Keep the group on track with strong yet gentle encouragement and guidance.

> *Connect:* Utilize the Connect activities to help group members share about what they know best—themselves—and to get them actively involved in the discussion. Take advantage of these creative learning activities. The main question here is "What is *your* story?"

> *Study:* These discussion questions are arranged to help members first observe and examine the Bible text, then understand and discern what the Scripture means and how they relate to it personally. The question here is "What is God saying to *you* in this passage?"

> *Apply:* This is the most important meeting element. Make sure you move the group toward this part of the process. Here they will relate God's Word to their own everyday lives and decide what they will *do* with it. The question here is "How will I respond?"

> *Inversion—Going Beyond Discussion:* Each session ends with a challenge for your group to take an action step that lives out the particular focus for the day. Some of these service opportunities are relatively simple, and others will take some additional planning. The question here is "How are we going to *reach others* with God's truth in a practical way?"

Before the Next Meeting: All group members should read the next chapter in *Inverted* for the upcoming meeting. They may also look up Scripture passages if they like, but they do not need to do any other homework.

Leader's Between-Meeting Shepherding Ideas: A healthy, life-changing small group is more than just what happens during the meeting time. The leader should set an example by staying in contact with participants between meetings though phone calls, visits, e-mail, and personal letters or cards. The best groups are like close families who care for one another 24/7.

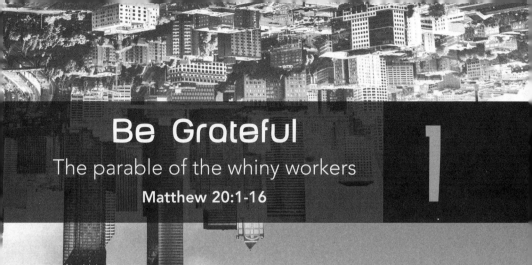

Be Grateful
The parable of the whiny workers
Matthew 20:1-16

Key word: *generous*—adjective meaning magnanimous, openhanded, liberal in giving
Antonyms: tightfisted, miserly

The Bottom Line: God can be as generous as he wants to be, because he is the owner of all. The truth is, God is more generous than we can imagine.

The Goal of This Session: To identify the single strand of truth in this parable. We will discover why fairness is not the focus and explain why the landowner could be "unfair" in his payment of his workers. We will select ways in which we can show our gratefulness by imitating God's generosity.

LEADER PREPARATION

Read Matthew 20:1-16, and Matthew 19:16-30 for setting the stage for this parable.

Read chapter 1 in the book *Inverted* by Tom Ellsworth.

Choose the activities and questions that best fit your group's style. Don't feel like your group must discuss every question.

Bring some kind of chocolate for the winner of the Gratitude Quotient opening activity.

Prepare name tags, stickers, or note cards—one for each person in your group. Write on each tag one of these starting times: 6 AM, 9 AM, 12 PM, 3 PM, 5 PM. (You may have multiples of the different times, depending on the number of people in your group.) Bring play money (such as money from a board game) to be distributed (in equal amounts) as payment to the "workers" in the Study exercise.

Pray that your group will get a glimpse of the magnitude of God's generosity and be compelled to emulate that attitude in their own lives.

CONNECT
My Experiences with Generosity

Choose one of these questions to answer and share with the group:

- Tell about a time when someone was unexpectedly generous toward you. How did that make you feel?
- Tell about how you learned to be a grateful person. Did you learn from a parent, a teacher, or from someone else? Did you have a good model or a not-so-great model of what it means to be grateful?
- Have you ever agreed to do a job, but you didn't know how much you were being paid? When you received the payment, were you pleased or disappointed? Why? Would you take on a job where the wage was uncertain? Why or why not?
- How would you categorize your reaction when someone extends generosity to you? Which one of the following statements are you most likely to think?

    a. Wow, I must be special!
    b. I didn't deserve that.
    c. I should look for a way to bless someone else the way I was blessed.

Gratitude Quotient

"I would maintain that thanks are the highest form of thought; and that gratitude is happiness doubled by wonder" (G. K. Chesterton, *A Short History of England*).

How grateful are you? Give yourself a point for each of the statements below that are true for you:

_____ I thanked a coworker today.
_____ I thanked a waiter/waitress today.
_____ I wrote a thank-you note this month. (Give yourself an extra point for each note you wrote.)
_____ I called someone to say thanks this week.
_____ I thanked a family member this week.
_____ I thanked a store clerk or person who bagged my groceries this week.

Give yourself ten points if this is true for you:

_____ I helped someone or gave something specifically because someone else had helped me.

Total your points and share your result with the group. The leader of the group can award a pat on the back (and some chocolate!) to the person with the highest gratitude quotient.

STUDY

1. The leader should begin by distributing the name tags or cards. A volunteer should read Matthew 19:30–20:16. When each start time is mentioned during the reading of the Bible story, the person(s) with that corresponding tag should stand up and stay standing. (Use 6 AM as the "early in the morning" start time, the "third hour" is 9 AM, the "sixth hour" is 12 PM, and so on.) After the reading, all group members should receive their pay from the leader. Then each "worker" can tell how he feels about the wage received.

2. Review the following phrases in the story describing the landowner. What can we learn about him from the text?

- He set up a payment arrangement with the first crew.
- He promised to pay later workers "whatever is right."
- He delegated to the foreman the task of distributing the payments.
- He instructed the foreman to start with the last ones hired.
- He called the protester "friend."
- He explained his right to pay whatever he wished to whomever he wanted.

What conclusions could you draw about the character and personality of the landowner? Who does the landowner represent?

LEADER'S NOTES

Here is some helpful background information concerning this parable.

When: Jesus told this story immediately following his encounter with the rich young ruler, and immediately before the triumphal entry into Jerusalem, the week before his death.

Who was in the audience: most likely his close disciples (see Matthew 19:23, 25, 27).

Why Jesus told this story: the disciples were astonished when Jesus told them it was nearly impossible for a rich man to enter the kingdom of Heaven. (The rich young ruler had just rejected Jesus.) Jews equated riches with God's favor. If the rich couldn't get in, who could?

Other Gospels where this parable is recorded: none.

Other Gospels where Jesus says, "The last will be first, and the first will be last": Mark 10:31; Luke 13:30.

3. In Matthew 19:30 this statement preceded the parable: "But many who are first will be last, and many who are last will be first." Jesus concluded the parable with, "So the last will be first, and the first will be last" (20:16). Why do you suppose that Jesus reversed the order of who got paid first?

4. What would you choose as the single strand of truth that Jesus is communicating in this parable? Why?

5. Compare these translations of the last part of Matthew 20:15. Which one makes it most clear for you? Why?

- "Or is your eye evil because I am good?" (*NKJV*) ("Is your eye evil?" is an idiom for jealousy or stinginess.)
- "Or are you envious because I am generous?" (*NIV*)
- "Should you be jealous because I am kind to others?" (*NLT*)
- "Are you going to get stingy because I am generous?" (*The Message*)

6. Jesus wasn't concerned in this parable with fairness in pay, or the quality of labor. Based on the disciples' question to Jesus in Matthew 19:25 and Peter's question in 19:27, what do you think Jesus *was* illustrating with his parable?

APPLY

7. What part or parts of this parable would you classify as *inverted*—the unexpected twist that gets the attention of the audience?

8. Imagine you are hearing this parable told for the first time. What part of it would bother you the most? Why?

9. In the book *Inverted*, author Tom Ellsworth listed some benefits of generosity (see p. 23). Generosity encourages, heals, and surprises. How have you personally experienced the benefit of generosity in one of these ways? What other benefits might result from generosity?

10. The opposite of generosity is stinginess. How does an attitude of gratitude help overcome stinginess? What practical ways have you discovered for dealing with our natural tendency to hold on to our resources?

11. The following quotation is attributed to John Wesley (1703–1791), the founder of Methodism:

> Do all the good you can,
> By all the means you can,
> In all the ways you can,
> In all the places you can,
> At all the times you can,
> To all the people you can,
> As long as ever you can.

How is the landowner in Jesus' parable a good example of this quote? What things do we need to work on so that we can better emulate this attitude in our lives?

"He is a wise man who does not grieve for the things which he has not, but rejoices for those which he has" (Epictetus, from *The Discourses*).

Let's revisit the Gratitude Quotient activity with which we began this session. Which of the following will you accomplish during the coming week?

_____ I will thank a coworker, or my boss for something specific.
_____ I will thank a waiter/waitress/clerk for something they are expected to do.
_____ I will write a thank-you note to someone.
_____ I will call someone on the phone to say thanks.
_____ I will thank a family member for something I often take for granted.
_____ Other: _____ .

"We are a clear reflection of our Father when we share what we have been given" (from *Inverted*, p. 23). Brainstorm practical ways your group could start a "wave of generosity" flowing through your community. Discuss how you could surprise a neighbor with

- a generous gift of flowers;
- food;
- an offer to watch their kids;
- a secret lawn-mowing service;
- an undercover car-washing operation.

Before the next meeting read chapter 2 in *Inverted*. Review the principles for understanding parables in the introduction of Tom Ellsworth's book.

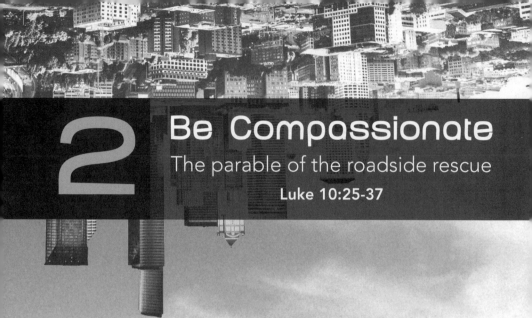

2 Be Compassionate
The parable of the roadside rescue
Luke 10:25-37

Key word: *compassion*—noun meaning sympathetic consciousness of others' distress, empathy, kindheartedness
Antonyms: coldness, indifference, apathy

The Bottom Line: Examine the compassion level in your heart. Do you care more about simply fulfilling the law or about serving the one in need, regardless of the risks and consequences?

The Goal of This Session: To expand our view of our neighborhood and enlarge our capacity for compassion. We will imagine the excuses offered by the "religious right" in this parable and will evaluate our own excuses for our lack of involvement. We will learn to recognize what stirs each of us to take compassionate action and plan ways to capitalize on those situations and feelings. We will estimate the size of our own comfort zones and plan ways to expand our willingness to show compassion in uncomfortable settings.

Read Luke 10:25-37.

Read chapter 2 in the book *Inverted* by Tom Ellsworth.

Food for thought: Read "A Bad Samaritan," by Teshelle Combs, *Relevant Magazine*, July 27, 2010 (http://www.relevantmagazine.com/god/deeper-walk/blog/22385-a-bad-samaritan).

Pray that this familiar story will pierce the hearts of your group for deeper impact, causing them to serve someone in Jesus' name in a tangible way.

CONNECT
How Big Is Your Comfort Zone?
As you begin, share your responses to the following questions:

- When was the last time you were out of your comfort zone in the arena of helping others?
- Were you forced to be uncomfortable, or did you venture out voluntarily? What happened?
- Would you describe your comfort zone as expanding or stagnant? Explain your answer.

Brainstorm with the group to compile some ways a person could expand his or her comfort zone.

Roadside Rescue
Group members can take turns sharing their responses to these questions: Have you ever been involved in a roadside rescue? Did you assist someone? How? Did you receive help from someone? What happened?

If you were on the giving—not receiving—end, what factors helped you decide to stop and get involved?

STUDY

1. Guess which of these would *not* go with the phrase *Good Samaritan*: law, society, hospital, parable, movie, legislation about clean water. (See Leader's Notes for answer.)

2. Someone in the group should read Luke 10:25-37 aloud. While this is happening, four different people should keep track of the actions (indicated by verbs) of each of the characters in the story: the robbers, the priest, the Levite, and the Samaritan. Each person can keep track of a different character or group. Use the chart below to do so.

Robbers	Priest	Levite	Samaritan

Do the priest and the Levite have more (actions and attitudes) in common with the robbers, or with the Samaritan? What insights can we gain from this?

3. Suggest some excuses that the priest or Levite might have offered about why they did not help the injured man. Francis Schaeffer said, "There is nothing more ugly than a Christian orthodoxy without understanding or without compassion" (*The God Who Is There*). What do you think Jesus wanted his listeners to see about the actions of these men?

LEADER'S NOTES

Jericho had become a priestly city where priests lived when they were not on duty in Jerusalem (G. Campbell Morgan, *Parables and Metaphors of Our Lord* [Old Tappan, NJ: Revell, 1943], 178). This implies that the priest and Levite were off duty—on their way home from service in Jerusalem.

If the victim were already dead, the priest and the Levite both would have defiled themselves by touching the body. They would have been required to undergo ceremonial cleansing, separating them from their duties for a week (Craig L. Blomberg, *Preaching the Parables* [Grand Rapids: Baker, 2004], 61).

Answer to Study question 1: Surprise! All of these items are connected to the term *Good Samaritan*. This is one Bible story that is known across cultures and generations.

4. Match the people category below with the topic on the right that was important to them.

the lawyer   compassion
the Jewish audience   the law
the Savior   prejudice against another culture

Which one of the three topics listed tends to dominate more of your thought processes? Be honest.

5. Read the Scripture verses listed below. In each situation, what moved Jesus to show compassion? What actions did he take?

Matthew 9:35, 36

Matthew 14:13, 14, 19-21

Matthew 20:29-34

Mark 1:40-42

What other examples can you suggest where Jesus treated people with compassion?

APPLY

6. Pretend you are interviewing the Samaritan. What do you imagine he would he say when you asked him why he, a Samaritan, would take a risk, offer first aid, and spend his money to get involved with a Jew?

7. Pretend you are interviewing the injured man. How do you think he felt about being rescued and cared for by a Samaritan? Do you think his attitude toward Samaritans would change? Why or why not? Do you think he would be more likely to stop and help someone else? Why or why not?

8. Norman Cousins said, "The individual is capable of both great compassion and great indifference. He has it within his means to nourish the former and outgrow the latter" (*The Celebration of Life*). After helping someone, how can you continue serving with compassion, instead of feeling proud of your accomplishment or looking for gratitude from the person you helped? How do you nourish compassion?

9. Read Leviticus 19:15, 18. When faced with an opportunity to love your neighbor as yourself, do you tend to think too highly of yourself ("I understand this situation and I know how to fix it") or do you tend to think too lowly of yourself ("I might say or do the wrong thing; how embarrassing would that be")? How can we take steps to remove the focus from ourselves and simply let Jesus work through us?

10. In *Inverted*, author Tom Ellsworth asks, "How many times has your plan to serve God prevented you from God's plan for you to serve?" Share honest responses to this question as God prompts you. Why do you suppose in his parable Jesus chose to have the men who ignored the injured man be people for whom religion was part of their profession? Why didn't he use a farmer and a fisherman?

11. We can almost imagine the Samaritan saying "My heart went out to him," as he later told about helping the beaten traveler. What makes your heart go out to someone? What stirs your compassion: hungry children, the homeless, elderly people who are lonely, kids without a father, those suffering from ongoing depression, special needs children or adults? Share with the group your completion of this sentence: "I really have a heart for _____ ." Tell a little bit about how that connection developed.

12. Is it OK to simply *prepare* to be compassionate if a need intersects with your path? Why or why not? How far should Christians go to intentionally seek out opportunities to show compassion to others?

Open Our Eyes

Talk with your group about watching this week for someone in your path who could use the touch of a Good Samaritan. What could you do to prepare to help someone?

- Get some grocery or gas gift cards to carry with you.
- Pack an extra lunch and water bottle for a homeless person you pass on the way to work.
- Other ideas?

Pray that you will notice and respond to the people God puts in your path.

Walking Wounded

Where can you find the hurting people in your community? Contact a local mental health center. Ask about how you can be a blessing to a family or individual who suffers from ongoing depression. Contact the VFW in your town. Find out how you could assist a wounded veteran.

Before the next meeting read chapter 3 in *Inverted*.

Be Forgiving
The parable of the shocking servant
Matthew 18:21-35

3

Key word: *forgive*—verb meaning to pardon, excuse, overlook; to cease to feel resentment

Antonyms: punish, call for payment, hold a grudge, seek revenge

The Bottom Line: God will never ask us to forgive anybody more than we've already been forgiven by our Father.

The Goal of This Session: To seek God's grace as a starting place for dealing with forgiveness. We will examine the nearly incomparable difference between the two debts in the parable. We will increase our personal awareness of how much God has poured forgiveness into our lives—and celebrate it! And we will consider how to strengthen our willingness to forgive others.

LEADER PREPARATION

Read Matthew 18:21-35.

Read chapter 3 in the book *Inverted* by Tom Ellsworth.

Prepare an index card for each person in your group. First, write this phrase across the center in black or blue pen: "My Big Ugly Debts." Next, use a red pen or marker and write over the first phrase diagonally "Paid in Full."

Pray for God to prepare the hearts of those in your group who may be carrying large burdens of unforgiveness.

CONNECT
Forgiveness Training

Think back to your childhood. Each person should choose one or two of these questions to answer and share answers with the group:

- How did your parents teach you about forgiveness?
- What did they tell you to say when asking forgiveness from someone you had hurt?
- Did the phrase "Say it like you mean it!" get used much in your home? How so?
- Did your parents ever ask you to forgive them? What happened?
- Did people in your family hold grudges? Was it easy or difficult to feel forgiven? Why?
- Would you say that your childhood gave you an above average, average, or poor preparation for forgiving others as an adult? Explain.

Irreconcilable Differences

Match the person or people group in the left column with their mortal enemy (enemies) in the second column.

Queen Elizabeth I	Bugs Moran
Ephraim Hatfield	Sunnis
Al Capone	Palestinians
Aaron Burr	Alexander Hamilton
Shiites	Protestants of Northern Ireland
Israelis	Mary Queen of Scots
Irish Catholics	William McCoy

Discuss as a group some ways in which lives and kingdoms and nations are torn apart when forgiveness is not practiced.

STUDY

1. When Peter asked Jesus how many times to forgive someone, what answer do you think Peter was expecting from Jesus?

2. Compare the first two scenes in the parable Jesus told. Review Matthew 18:23-29, and fill in the blanks below. Use modern-day equivalents for the amounts owed. Refer to pages 45–47 in *Inverted* for that information.

Debt holder	Debtor	Amount owed	Debtor's posture	Plea
king	first servant			
first servant	second servant			

3. Which debt was completely impossible to repay, and what debt does that represent in our lives?

4. What is a glaring difference in the way the king treated the first servant and the way the first servant treated the second servant in verse 28?

5. What attributes and characteristics of God are presented in verse 27?

6. How did the king react to the news about the servant he had forgiven? Do you think he was too harsh? Why or why not? How is the depiction of God in verses 32-34 different from the characteristics portrayed in verse 27?

7. Why does Jesus say that God will not forgive you unless you forgive others? See also Matthew 6:12, 14, 15; Mark 11:25.

8. Have volunteers read these verses aloud. Which of these verses reminding us of God's forgiveness makes the most impact on you? Why? How do you maintain your awareness of God's mercy toward you?

- Psalm 32:1, 2
- Psalm 103:10-12
- Isaiah 55:7
- Micah 7:18, 19
- Romans 8:1

LEADER'S NOTES

One hundred denarii is an amount of money that could be carried in a man's pocket (although not many men in Jesus' day would have trousers with pockets). The 10,000 talents would require 8,600 men, each carrying sixty pounds of sixpence coins in a backpack. If the men were spaced three feet apart, the line would be five miles long (William Barclay, *The Gospel of Matthew,* Volume 2 [Philadelphia: Westminster Press, 1975], 194).

It is possible that the debt of the first servant came through embezzlement. It is unlikely that the servant could have accumulated the massive debt without the master knowing about it. The servant must have been in a responsible position with access to the master's accounts. He apparently had used his position to steal from the master (Jennifer Kennedy Dean, *Secrets Jesus Shared* [Birmingham, AL: New Hope Publishers, 2007], 194).

APPLY

9. God does not have a forgiveness scale, making it so we don't have to forgive really heinous crimes like child abuse or rape. Why do you suppose God didn't create a scale like that? Why does he insist that we forgive, whether the offense is huge or small?

10. In his book *Forgive and Forget*, Lewis Smedes says that in forgiving you "set a prisoner free, but you discover that the real prisoner was yourself." One crucial activity in the process of forgiving is repeatedly handing over the offender to God, putting God in charge of justice. Read these verses:

- Romans 12:19
- 1 Peter 2:23
- 1 John 2:11, 12

How can it be liberating to put God in charge of the offender and his possible punishment?

11. In *What's So Amazing About Grace*, Philip Yancey wrote, "I have to approach God again and again, yielding to him the residue of what I thought I had committed to him long ago. . . . Only by living in the stream of God's grace will I find the strength to respond with grace toward others."

Which of the following thought processes or actions helps you most when you are extending forgiveness to others?

- Reminding myself how much God has forgiven me.
- Realizing that forgiveness is more for my benefit than for my offender.
- Remembering that extending forgiveness doesn't necessarily require reestablishing the relationship.
- Recognizing that forgiveness does not erase or negate the hurt that took place.
- Understanding that forgiveness does not necessarily cancel consequences for the offender.
- Recalling that extending forgiveness is an ongoing part of life, not a one-time event.
- Choosing to make forgiveness a God-controlled action that is not dictated by my feelings.

Share your ideas with the group. Some in your group may have walked further down the path of extending forgiveness. Let them share what has helped them learn to trust God in this process.

12. Have each person take one of the "Debt" cards. Allow several moments of quiet meditation. Consider what details might be included if you were to write out the meaning of "My Big Ugly Debts." Keep this card where you will see it daily for the next few weeks. Offer a prayer of gratitude for the fullness and long-lasting impact of God's forgiveness. Then, all this week, pray about your need to grow in the grace of forgiveness.

INVERSION > GOING BEYOND DISCUSSION

Consider contacting your local police department or district attorney's office to learn about restorative justice in your community. Someone in your group may be inspired to receive training to become a victim's advocate or to help in other programs that may be available.

Forgiveness Tree
What would happen if you "planted" a forgiveness tree in your church lobby or foyer? Chat with your church leadership about how this could work. Bring

in an artificial tree (even a small tabletop tree will work). Provide a stack of green cards, a stack of red cards, envelopes that are appropriately sized for the cards, and yarn or string for tying the envelopes in the tree. Prepare a small poster with these instructions:

Forgiveness Tree
If you need forgiveness for an offense you have committed, write a note to God on a red card. Remember 1 John 1:9, "If we confess our sins, he is faithful and just and will forgive us our sins."

If you need to forgive someone, write a note to God on a green card, asking for his help in the process. Remember Colossians 3:13, "Bear with each other and forgive whatever grievances you may have against one another. Forgive as the Lord forgave you."

Place your card in an envelope and fasten it to the tree. Ask God to lighten the burden you may have been carrying. Listen for him to direct you about asking for or giving forgiveness to the person involved. What you write here will remain confidential.

Plan for the tree to remain in place for two or three weekends. Then your group could pray over these requests (without reading the specifics of them).

For Further Study
Check out this website, http://theforgivenessproject.com. You'll find a moving collection of stories and ideas about restorative justice.

Some other helpful resources include *Getting Rid of the Gorilla: Confessions on the Struggle to Forgive*, by Brian Jones (Standard Publishing, 2008), and *Cultivating a Forgiving Heart: Forgiveness Frees Us to Flourish*, by Denise George (Zondervan, 2004). If you have more work to do in this area of forgiveness, these books will be very helpful.

Before the next meeting read chapter 4 in *Inverted*.

4 Be Gracious

The parable of the warmest welcome

Luke 15:11-32

> **Key word:** *prodigal*—adjective meaning profuse, exuberant, lavish; noun meaning waster, squanderer, spender, high roller
> **Antonyms:** parsimonious, stingy

If *prodigal* is used to refer to the son in Jesus' parable, the meaning is squanderer, one who wastes. If *prodigal* is used to refer to the Father in the story, the meaning is one who spent lavishly, exuberantly. Both disregarded the cost.

The Bottom Line: Jesus' story shows us the kind of Father we've always wanted, and what he wants for us too.

The Goal of This Session: To realize that God welcomes home those who want to come to him. We will adjust our attitudes concerning people we feel who are, or are not, deserving of God's grace. We will consider ways in which we have ignored or wasted God's grace in our lives. And we will choose a way to practice stop-drop-and-roll repentance in our lives.

Read Luke 15:11-32 and Luke 15:1-10 for context.

Read chapter 4 in the book *Inverted* by Tom Ellsworth.

Choose the activities and questions that best fit your group's style. Don't feel like your group must discuss every question.

Bring a laptop and display images of the prodigal son—artistic depictions of this parable that have been painted throughout the centuries. (Or go to the library and look up examples to bring.)

Pray that your excitement about a Father whose love goes over the top will show through during your discussion. Pray that those who already know this story will consider the message anew with an open heart.

CONNECT
School of Hard Knocks

As you begin, have group members discuss one of these questions:

- Have you ever squandered anything? blown a chance, missed an opportunity? Tell the group about it.
- Would you categorize yourself as a slow learner? That is, do you usually have to learn life lessons the hard way—by messing up first and then having to correct your actions? Tell the group about a time when you had to learn your lesson the hard way.
- Two-by-Four Therapy: You have heard people say something like, "God had to hit me over the head with a two-by-four for me to pay attention." Tell the group about your own two-by-four experience.

Family Feuds

On the next page, match the fathers with their sons. Look at the end of the Leader's Notes for the answers. (Numbers represent how many sons.)

Fathers

Joseph (3) Lloyd (2) Martin (3) Charles (2) Archie (2) George (4)

Sons

	George		William		Teddy		Eli
Harry		Jeff		Ramon		Jeb	
	Beau		Neil		Peyton		Jack
Emilio		Charlie		Marvin		Bobby	

How many of these families are famous for not getting along? Where is the conflict—father–son or brother–brother? What would you guess to be the leading causes of family feuds?

STUDY

Read Luke 15:11-32 as a drama. Use four readers: a narrator, a younger son, a father, and an older son.

1. Take an informal poll. Who are the two members of your group who are probably least familiar with this story? Ask for their reactions and impressions first.

2. Read Luke 15:1, 2. What two groups wanted to hear Jesus? What two groups wanted to criticize him? What problem did they have with Jesus?

3. Do you think a certain character in the parable represents the tax collectors and sinners? If so, which one? Do you think a certain character in the parable represents the Pharisees and teachers of the law? If so, which one? Explain your answers.

4. In your opinion, was the father wise or foolish in giving the younger son his portion of the estate? Why?

Jewish tradition was rigid about inheritance. Typically it was distributed upon the death of the father, and not before. The younger son in this parable essentially said, "For all I care, you're dead. I just want your money." The father damaged his reputation by carrying out the son's request (Dean, 120–21).

According to Old Testament law (Deuteronomy 21:17), the firstborn son received a double portion of his father's estate. So the older brother would have had twice as much as the younger (A.T. Robertson, *Word Pictures in the New Testament*, Vol. 2 [Nashville: Broadman, 1930], 207).

Answers to the Family Feuds match-up:

- Joseph Kennedy: Jack, Bobby, Teddy
- Lloyd Bridges: Beau, Jeff
- Martin Sheen: Charlie, Emilio, Ramon
- Prince Charles: Harry, William
- Archie Manning: Eli, Peyton
- George Herbert Walker Bush: George, Jeb, Neil, Marvin

5. Why do you suppose the son didn't head for home as soon as he ran out of money?

6. Are you surprised that the son declared, "I have sinned against heaven"? What do you think he meant by saying that?

7. The two parables that precede this one (the lost sheep and the lost coin) both have a similar phrase, "There is rejoicing in the presence of the angels of God over one sinner who repents." What scene in this parable presents a parallel thought?

8. Review the unusual twists in this story that would have surprised the Jewish audience:

- The son asked for his inheritance before his father died.
- The father gave the son his inheritance, although he was not required to do so.
- The Jewish son took a job feeding pigs.
- The father threw a party and reinstated the son who had wasted his inheritance.
- The older brother stayed home working with the father but didn't adopt his father's gracious viewpoint toward the prodigal.

How do we learn that the father cared as much about the older brother as he did for the younger?

Read 2 Corinthians 12:15. How does this verse represent the attitude of the father?

9. Make a list of the ways that the father in the story is like God. Share with the group the one that is your favorite and why. How does this parable illustrate the principle of mercy triumphing over judgment (James 2:13)?

10. Jesus described the turning point in the prodigal's attitude with the words, "He came to his senses." Repentance has been described as a Stop-Drop-and-Roll activity:

- *Stop* what you are doing.
- *Drop* to your knees and tell God you are sorry.
- *Roll*—turn your life 180 degrees and head in the opposite direction.

Complete the following chart: first use the verses from the text to trace the son's actions of repentance, then record your own faith journey.

Repentance	Younger Son	Me
Stop	v. 17	
Drop	vv. 18, 19	
Roll	vv. 20, 21	

For more study on repentance, check out Luke 15:7; Acts 2:38, 3:19, 17:30; Romans 2:4; 2 Corinthians 7:10; Revelation 2:5.

11. You might have been raised in a religious tradition where repentance was viewed as one step in the salvation process—something you did in order to receive salvation. Why is that an inadequate view? How would you explain to someone that repenting is an ongoing discipline in a Christian's life?

APPLY

12. The son came to his senses when he: 1) ran out of money; 2) took a disgusting job; 3) was so hungry he would have eaten pig slop. What has it taken for you to "come to your senses" in the area of repentance? In what ways was your moment of enlightenment similar to—or different from—the younger son's experience?

13. When the son came to his senses, he repented and went back home, willing to be a servant. Complete the sentence, "When I came to my senses, I repented and _____ ."

14. Which son do you tend to be like most of the time? Why? Which of these is more applicable to you?

_____ I need to come to my senses and accept the love God is offering me. "Wise up and leave the stupidity of sin far behind. Turn around and head for home" (*Inverted*, p. 63).

_____ I need to get over being resentful and judgmental and let God's love flow through me to others. "Be gracious; there is no better way to surprise a justice-hungry world than with the forgiveness of God" (*Inverted*, p. 69).

INVERSION > GOING BEYOND DISCUSSION

Challenge yourself to volunteer for a task that you are uncomfortable doing. If you are shy, try being a greeter before church. If you fear elderly people, why not visit an assisted living center? If you usually serve at church, help out at a food kitchen. Commit to doing more than one service project; commit to a month focused on serving.

- Journal your feelings and observations about how the experience causes you to "come to your senses."

- What did you learn about God, the loving Father, and about yourself?

- Find a way to offer kindness to someone whom you might consider undeserving, like the prodigal—a homeless person, an offender serving a sentence in a local jail, etc.

- For more about how to help and when not to help, read *When Helping Hurts: How to Alleviate Poverty Without Hurting the Poor . . . and Yourself*, by Brian Fikkert and Steve Corbett (Moody, 2009).

Before the next meeting read chapter 5 in *Inverted*.

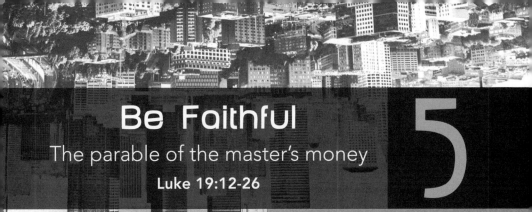

Be Faithful
The parable of the master's money
Luke 19:12-26

5

Key word: *faithful*—adjective meaning dependable, reliable, trustworthy, reso-
lute, steadfast, devoted
Antonyms: faithless, traitorous, unstable, perfidious, fickle, wavering

The Bottom Line: Loyal obedience pleases the king more than outra-
geous success.

The Goal of This Session: To increase our faithfulness to God. We
will acknowledge God's right to expect faithfulness from his followers. We
will discover that Jesus was preparing his followers for faithfulness to him
after he returned to Heaven. We will celebrate God's faithfulness toward us.
And individually, we will expand our willingness to work at being faithful.

LEADER PREPARATION

Read Luke 19:11-26.

Read chapter 5 in the book *Inverted* by Tom Ellsworth.

Review the chart on page 39 comparing two similar but unique parables.

You'll want to be familiar with the Parable of the Talents, so that if group members mix the elements of the parables you can keep the discussion on track.

Pray about your own faithfulness to God. Ask him to show you the small areas in your life that need attention.

CONNECT
Faithful and Unfaithful Examples

Divide your group in half. Let someone be the timer. Each subgroup should take about three or four minutes to make a list of names that fit the following categories:

- A faithful canine companion
- A faithful Native American companion
- A faithful friend from the Bible
- A faithful wife or husband
- A famous traitor
- An infamous and faithless wife or husband
- A corrupt politician
- A businessman who stole from his company

After the designated time is up, each group should reveal its list. Eliminate any answers you have that are duplicates. Offer a round of applause for the group with the most answers.

Discuss: What kinds of attitudes and actions are present in a person who is known as being faithful?

Setting a Pattern for Faithfulness

Depending on the amount of time you have available, discuss some of the following questions:

- Did you ever get in trouble as a child for not completing a chore assigned to you? What kind of discipline did you receive? How did you learn your lesson?
- What's the shortest time span you stuck with a sport, hobby, or music lessons that you tried? What's the longest time span you've devoted to such a pursuit?

- What is the longest amount of time you have spent cultivating a friendship? What have been two or three major keys to keeping that relationship going?

STUDY

1. Read the parable aloud, including the introduction in verse 11. As Jesus headed toward Jerusalem, what were his disciples expecting to happen?

2. What did the master expect from his servants according to verse 13?

3. Do you think that the master was giving the cities and their profits to the first two servants as rewards, or was he giving the servants a promotion—responsibility to manage the cities for the master? Explain your answer.

4. What excuses did the third servant give for not multiplying his money from the master? Do you think his excuses were valid? Why or why not? What other motivation could he have had?

LEADER'S NOTES

Jesus applied this parable to himself to show that what the crowds were expecting would not take place. He was going to Jerusalem, but not to receive a kingdom. Forty days after the resurrection he would leave them with responsibility to carry out the kingdom (Morgan, 245–46).

The root word for *handkerchief,* or "piece of cloth," in verse 20 is *sweat,* as in sweat rag (Robertson, 242).

5. In your opinion, was the master harsh and demanding as the third servant described? What do the master's interactions with the other servants tell you about him?

6. What part of the parable predicts the outcome of Jesus' kingdom?

7. Divide your group into two subgroups. (Use the same groups from earlier if you opened with the competitive activity.) Allow about eight minutes for groups to prepare their lists that they will share.

Group 1: *God's Faithfulness to Us.* Using the Scriptures below, list some things that indicate what God's faithfulness means for us. Include examples of God's faithfulness to specific people in the Bible.

Deuteronomy 7:7-9

Psalm 86:15

Lamentations 3:22, 23

1 Corinthians 10:13

2 Thessalonians 3:3

Group 2: *Our Faithful Response to God.* Using the Scriptures below, list some ways in which we can demonstrate our faithfulness to God. Include examples of how specific people in the Bible proved their faithfulness to God.

Joshua 24:14, 15

1 Samuel 12:24, 25

1 Corinthians 4:1, 2

Hebrews 10:22-25

1 Peter 4:10, 11

Revelation 2:10

A Comparison Between Two Similar Parables

Parable	Ten Minas	Talents
Reference	Luke 19:11-27	Matthew 25:14-30
Appears when?	right before triumphal entry	3-4 days later
Where told?	leaving Jericho	Jerusalem
Why told?	verse 11: show delay in kingdom; need for faithfulness	show need for responsibility and faithfulness
Who gives money?	man going to be appointed king; subjects hated him	man on a journey
Number of servants?	ten	three
Distribution?	equal: one mina per person	unequal: five, two, and one
Worth?	100 days' wages	large amount
Report from?	only three servants	all three servants
Reward given?	cities	verbal praise: "Well done good and faithful" put in charge of more
What the unfaithful did?	hid money in sweat rag	buried money in ground
Excuses?	you are a hard man reap what you did not sow I was afraid	you are a hard man harvesting without sowing I was afraid
Master's response?	wicked take away mina give to one with ten	judge you by your words wicked, lazy take away talent give to one with ten
Jesus' summary?	more given to one who has one with nothing will lose that	everyone who has will be given more
Master's verdict?	kill enemies in front of me	whoever has nothing, that will be taken from him throw out worthless servant into darkness and weeping

APPLY

8. If you had been a servant in this parable, would you have been thrilled for the opportunity to multiply the master's money or would you have been terrified? Why?

9. How do you rate yourself as a risk taker for God? Are you cautious and careful, because you might make a mistake? Are you brave and bold, because God's got your back? Or are you somewhere in between? Place a mark on the line below that describes how you view yourself when it comes to being adventurous for God.

cautious and careful   brave and bold

What would it take for you to move farther down the right side of the line?

10. Review the list of simple Bible commands on page 80 of *Inverted*. How many of these are easy for you? How many of them are difficult? Choose one that you will focus on to faithfully obey as you go throughout the coming week.

11. Do you exhibit any of the symptoms of Third-Servant Syndrome? Examine yourself honestly. Could you have even a mild case of this dangerous condition? Check all the symptoms that apply to you:

☐ Nauseating complacency: lackadaisical attitude toward responsibilities.

☐ Fractured excuses: defensive and full of alibis and explanations.

☐ Feverish spite: angry at God for not carrying out your wishes on your timetable.

Suggest a possible remedy for each symptom.

Give out some awards or recognition to some in your church family who have exhibited faithfulness in these and other ways:

- They have cleaned the church building for a long time.
- They have served in the nursery.
- They have served as youth and children's workers.
- They have faithfully visited shut-ins.
- They have worked in ministries that serve the developmentally disabled.
- They help park cars and transport people in good weather and bad.

These folks usually don't like the spotlight. Be on the lookout for people who work behind the scenes. You may bless them the most by sending a card you all have signed, or by taking a road trip from house to house to deliver flowers, homemade cookies, and to give hugs of appreciation for their faithfulness.

Before the next meeting read chapter 6 in *Inverted*.

6

Be Authentic

The parable of the pompous and pious prayers

Luke 18:9-14

Key word: *authentic*—adjective meaning real, actual, true, transparent, vulnerable, genuine

Antonyms: fake, deceptive, pretend, hypocrite, phony, fraud, impostor

---

The Bottom Line: The heart of this story is not about talking to God, but about being authentic in the presence of God and others.

The Goal of This Session: To open ourselves up to God's desire to produce authenticity in our lives. We will discover from their prayers how the two main characters viewed God, themselves, and others. We will evaluate our willingness to be authentic and then individually select an area in which we will concentrate on developing more authenticity.

LEADER PREPARATION

Read Luke 18:9-14. Also read Jesus' strong words to and about the Pharisees in Luke 11:39-52 and Matthew 23:1-7, 13-33.

Read chapter 6 in the book *Inverted* by Tom Ellsworth.

CONNECT
Certificate of Authenticity

Certificates of authenticity sometimes accompany products. They guarantee verification from the seller. They are used for coins, antiques, gems, works of art, and many other high-end products. When you have one, you can be sure that your purchase is genuine, original, and authentic—not a knockoff.

Wouldn't it be great if Christians came with a certificate of authenticity? Then you would be able to spot the fakes instantly.

With your group, brainstorm a list of things you look for in people to know if their walk with God is genuine. What are some red flags that might concern you?

Infamous Fakes

"You can fool some of the people all of the time, and all of the people some of the time, but you cannot fool all of the people all the time" (this quotation has been attributed to both Abraham Lincoln and P. T. Barnum). Some have been more successful at fooling people than others. Match the person with the life they pretended to live. Correct answers are at the end of this session.

_____ Anna Anderson
_____ David Hampton
_____ Dave Kovic
_____ Frank Abagnale
_____ Mary Baker
_____ Chevalier d'Éon
_____ Perkin Warbeck

a. Succeeded in pretending to be a Pan Am pilot, a pediatrician, a Harvard-trained lawyer, and a professor. He was played by Leonardo DiCaprio in the movie *Catch Me If You Can*.

b. Claimed to be the Grand Duchess Anastasia, daughter of Czar Nicholas II.

c. Posed as the son of actor Sidney Poitier. The film *Six Degrees of Separation* was based on him.

d. In the movie titled by his first name, starring Kevin Kline and Sigourney Weaver, he is hired as a stand-in for the president, and eventually takes his place.

e. Spoke in a made-up language and posed as Princess Caraboo, supposedly swam ashore near Bristol, England, and said she had escaped from pirates.

f. Hanged in 1499 for pretending to be Richard, Duke of York, youngest son of Edward IV. Mary Shelley, author of Frankenstein, wrote a fictionalized account of his life.

g. French diplomat and spy. Lived the first half of life as a man, the second as a woman. Bram Stoker wrote about this person in his book, *Famous Impostors*.

If you know the stories of any of these impostors, share with the group how the person got away with the deception. What made the impostor seem authentic?

STUDY

1. Read through the parable, then discuss these questions about the two characters.

   The Pharisee

   - According to verse 11, what did he pray about?
   - To whom was he praying?
   - For whose benefit was he praying?
   - For what was he thankful?
   - What did he include in his report to God of good behavior?

   The Tax Collector

   - What do you think it means in verse 13 that "he stood at a distance"? What was he trying to be far from?

- Where was he looking? Why?
- What message was he sending by "beating his breast"?
- What did he request from God?
- How did he view himself?

2. In this parable the audience would have expected _____ to be the good guy, because _____ . The audience would have expected _____ to be the bad guy, because _____ .

3. What was wrong with the Pharisee's prayer? Given that he believed God to be very pleased with his performance, describe the kind of God he expected God to be.

4. What is right with the tax collector's prayer? What would please God about this man's prayer? Based on his seven-word prayer, describe the kind of God he expected to hear his prayer.

5. Brainstorm some ways that the Pharisee and the tax collector were polar opposites in their actions, words, and attitudes. Look on pages 96-99 in *Inverted* for ideas.

6. Jesus concluded the parable with this principle: "Everyone who exalts himself will be humbled, and he who humbles himself will be exalted." Read Luke 14:7-11. How is the point of this second parable similar to the one about the Pharisee and the tax collector?

Compare the wording of Luke 18:9 in several Bible translations:

- "confident of their own righteousness and looked down on everybody else" (*NIV*)

- "who had great confidence in their own righteousness and scorned everyone else" (*NLT*)

- "complacently pleased with themselves over their moral performance and looked down their noses at the common people" (*The Message*)

- "trusted in themselves that they were righteous, and despised others" (*NKJV*)

- "trusted in themselves that they were righteous, and viewed others with contempt" (*NASB*)

The word *contempt* carries with it a strong thought concerning rejection. This same Greek word is also used in Luke 23:11 (Herod and his soldiers treated Jesus with contempt and mocked him) and Romans 14:10 (Do not regard your brother with contempt).

The *New American Standard Bible* translates Luke 18:13 as "God, be merciful to me, the sinner!" and is preferred by some scholars. They interpret the use of the article *the* as a way to emphasize how seriously the man felt about his sins. Compare to the way Paul felt about himself in 1 Timothy 1:15, 16 (Robertson, 233–34; R. C. Foster, *Studies in the Life of Christ* [Joplin: College Press, 1995], 1004).

APPLY

7. "The Pharisee offered a soliloquy disguised as a prayer. It was for the benefit of those around him" (Dean, 174). The Pharisee could easily focus on the sins and errors of those around him. Yet he was oblivious to his own pride and judgmental spirit. Read Matthew 7:3-5 and Psalm 24:3, 4. If you were prescribing a remedy to cure the Pharisee of his raging case of hypocrisy, what would you recommend?

8. If you were to receive an appraisal from "The Department of Spiritual Authenticity," how would you rate? Where would you place yourself on the continuum between these extremes?

Transparent _____ Masked

Honest _____ Deceptive

Aware of my weaknesses _____ Blind to my faults

Able to confess sins _____ Unwilling to open up

Able to consistently
tell the truth _____ Tend to stretch truth
or leave out parts

Able to resist
peer pressure _____ Mostly following
others' expectations

Not worried about
others' opinions _____ Mostly trying to make
a good impression

What are some other actions and attitudes of authenticity you might add to this list?

9. Telling the group how great you are doing with authenticity may win you a Pharisee award. Share what you feel comfortable sharing about your struggles with authenticity. Select an area that you want to work on with God's help.

10. Potential car buyers are urged to uncover the truth about a vehicle through the CARFAX vehicle history report. The report shows recurring problems, past accidents, the number of previous owners, and other

potential sources of trouble. While you might not want a car with previous damage or engine problems, it's a different story with people. The most compassionate friend might be someone who has gone through severe pain. A person who demonstrates a kind and peaceful heart may have overcome a nasty temper. An authentic life is not a perfect life, just one that is transparent and honest.

How do hard times and adversity peel away layers until the authentic person remains? How has that been true in your life? How can a person keep from becoming hardened and bitter, rather than authentic?

11. Many Christians resist accountability. They dislike having to report on a struggle. They would rather have the matter be between them and God. (Those people typically do not join a small group.) How does accountability strengthen authenticity? How has accountability to a friend or spouse helped you stay true to your purpose and calling?

12. Close by having several people in the group read the following verses aloud. Then each person can pray silently about allowing God to assist them with authenticity in their lives.

"I live in a high and holy place, but also with him who is contrite and lowly in spirit" (Isaiah 57:15).

"This is the one I esteem: he who is humble and contrite in spirit, and trembles at my word" (Isaiah 66:2).

"The LORD is close to the brokenhearted and saves those who are crushed in spirit" (Psalm 34:18).

This session's suggestion for a service project must be individually driven, not a group activity. When you choose to serve someone who cannot reciprocate, you choose authenticity. When you choose to serve in a situation where no one is going to pat you on the back or praise you, you choose authenticity. When you choose to serve when it is not convenient, when it is not neatly packaged, when you are not sure of how much may be demanded from you, you choose authenticity. When you choose to serve alone, without the encouragement of your friends or teammates, you choose authenticity. Commit yourself to find a secret place of unnoticed service, the sooner the better.

For Further Study

- *12 Steps for the Recovering Pharisee (like me)*, by John Fischer (Bethany House, 2000)

- *Who You Are When No One's Looking*, by Bill Hybels (InterVarsity Press, 1989)

Before the next meeting read chapter 7 in *Inverted*.

Answers to the Infamous Fakes activity:

b. Anna Anderson
c. David Hampton
d. Dave Kovic
a. Frank Abagnale
e. Mary Baker
g. Chevalier d'Éon
f. Perkin Warbeck

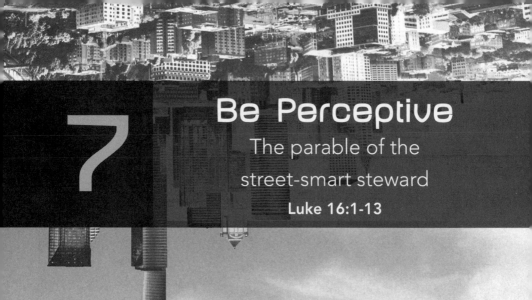

7

Be Perceptive
The parable of the
street-smart steward
Luke 16:1-13

Key word: *shrewd*—adjective meaning clever, savvy, canny, crafty; and often slick, given to wily and artful ways of dealing
Antonyms: foolish, unthinking, stupid, naïve

The Bottom Line: As the steward made the most of his opportunity, we need to be shrewd in our relationships with others and be wise about how we use the resources God has given us.

The Goal of This Session: To discover why Jesus used a dishonest steward as a positive example. We will recognize how the dishonest steward was shrewd, and how he was foolish. We will acknowledge the inadequacy of being only street-smart or book smart. And we will learn to be perceptive in our relationships and to take wise steps for preparing for an eternal future.

Read Luke 16:1-15.

Read chapter 7 in the book *Inverted* by Tom Ellsworth.

Pray that the difficulties in explaining some parts of this parable will not obscure Jesus' call to act with urgency.

CONNECT
Smartest/Dumbest
Choose one of the statements below to share with the group:

- Tell about the smartest or dumbest financial decision you've ever made.
- Tell about the smartest or dumbest relationship decision you've ever made.
- Tell about the smartest or dumbest job-related decision you've ever made.

Are you more street-smart or book-smart? When is it better to be street-smart? When is it better to be book-smart?

What kind of boss would you rather have—street-smart or book-smart? Why?

People Are Like That
How many of these hypothetical people resemble someone you know or have heard about? Put a check mark beside each description of a person that you know.

_____ I know someone who, when faced with a problem, spends more time blaming others and finding excuses than seeking a solution.

_____ I know someone who will invest in classes and training so he or she can be eligible for a promotion, but this person cannot be bothered to regularly read the Bible.

_____ I know someone who spends hours every week perfecting a sport or a hobby, but who has no time to memorize Scripture or improve communication skills.

_____ I know someone who spends more time preparing for a vacation than for eternity.

_____ I know someone who spends more on his or her own pleasures than this person spends to help hurting, hungry people.

_____ I know someone who gets more excited about a sports team than about church participation.

As we study and discuss the parable of the street-smart steward, prepare to compare these examples with the message of the parable.

STUDY
Read aloud verses 1-7.

1. The master heard that his steward could possibly be cheating him. Suggest two or three responses he could have made. Which one did he choose?

2. The steward learned that his master thought he had cheated and had planned to fire him. Suggest two or three responses he could have made. Which one did he choose?

3. The master then heard that the steward had cheated him again and had reduced the debts of his customers. Suggest two or three responses he could have made. Which one did he choose?

4. What was the steward's motivation for reducing the debtors' bills? (See verse 4.)

Read aloud verses 8-15.

5. Who commended the dishonest steward? In your opinion was the steward commended for his dishonest behavior or for some other reason? Explain.

6. According to verse 15, how would God view dishonest behavior?

7. Tom Ellsworth wrote, "Jesus' words bring to mind a stinging realization: the people of this world give more thought to their physical well-being than the people of light do to their spiritual well-being" (*Inverted*, p. 110). In what way was Jesus saying, "Be like this steward"?

8. It doesn't seem very likely that Jesus was telling people to use money to buy friends (verse 9). What was he saying about the use of money? What was he saying about the importance of relationships?

9. It doesn't seem very likely that Jesus was telling us to use our money "wisely" so that we can earn ourselves a nice eternal dwelling. What was he saying in verses 10-13? Read Matthew 10:16, where the word *shrewd* is used in the *NIV*. How does this verse add to the understanding of the parable?

10. Read beyond the end of the parable, in verses 14 and 15. How did the Pharisees respond to the parable? How does the description of the Pharisees and their reaction to this parable help us process the point Jesus was making?

The steward was accused of wasting his master's possessions. The text does not tell us whether the manager was sloppy, careless, or dishonest. The same word for "wasting" was also used in Luke 15:13, where the younger son squandered his inheritance.

The steward is labeled *dishonest* in verse 8. The word means unrighteous, not upright, or unjust. That same word is used in verse 11 and is translated as worldly wealth.

Common New Testament words for money refer to silver or copper coins. The Greek word *ploutos*, meaning riches or wealth, is used over twenty times in the New Testament. It could refer to either physical money or to spiritual riches. Some of its occurrences include: Ephesians 1:7 (riches of God's grace); 1:18 (riches of his glory); 2:7 (incomparable riches of his grace); 3:8 (unsearchable riches of Christ); 3:16 (his glorious riches); Philippians 4:19 (his glorious riches in Christ); and James 5:2 (physical wealth).

The saying "you cannot serve both God and money" or, in some translations, "you cannot serve God and mammon" from Luke 16:13 also appears in Matthew 6:24. The word *mammon* is of Aramaic origin. It's used three times in this parable, in verses 9, 11, and 13. Some scholars treat *mammon* in the text as a personification, or "The Money God."

APPLY

11. The steward *ran out of time.* He might have thought he would have time to make things right, to put money back in the accounts. But the time was up.

Next, the steward *ran out of the master's trust.* When hearing the accusation, the master did not respond, "Not my servant, I am absolutely certain that he serves me honestly!" The steward had apparently used up his chances.

Then, the steward *ran out of options:* too weak to dig, too ashamed to beg, too old to start over somewhere else, and too fearful to go to prison. He saw no other option than to make a deal with the creditors.

Ultimately, the steward *ran out of vision*. His perspective and planning involved only the short term, nothing beyond this world.

How can we learn from his mistakes? Which one of these "ran out of" scenarios seems most applicable to your current situation? Explain.

12. Read these verses. How do they instruct us to wisely prepare for our spiritual future?

- Matthew 6:19-21
- Ephesians 5:15-17
- Colossians 4:5
- 1 Timothy 6:17-19
- James 4:13-17

13. David Paul Brown wrote, in his "Golden Rules for the Examination of Witnesses," "Be mild with the mild; shrewd with the crafty; confiding to the honest; merciful to the young, the frail, or the fearful; rough to the ruffian, and a thunderbolt to the liar. But in all this, never be unmindful of your own dignity. Bring to bear all the powers of your mind, not that *you* may shine, but that *virtue* may triumph, and your *cause* may prosper" (as quoted in Francis Wellman, *The Art of Cross-Examination* [Chicago: ABA Publishing, 2009], 233). What does this quote mean for you? Does it have any application to Christian life?

14. The phrases below correspond to sections of chapter 7 in *Inverted* (see pages 106–15). Read the Scriptures that accompany each idea. Select one action that you will focus on in order to make an eternal difference in your life. Share your choice with the group.

Hurry Up
John 4:35, 36

Galatians 6:10
Ephesians 5:16

Wise Up
Proverbs 2:3-6 (Pray for wisdom)
James 3:13-18 (Work at wisdom)
Colossians 1:10 (Grow in wisdom)

Look Up
Psalm 63:1-4

Show Up
Hebrews 10:23-25, 36

Stand Up
Philippians 3:12-14

INVERSION > GOING BEYOND DISCUSSION

Let's focus on the phrase from this parable, "Use worldly wealth to gain friends."

• Could your group invest in a family in your church or neighborhood?

• Is there a single mom whose car needs repairs?

• What about an elderly person who needs a porch repaired?

• How could you make it possible for a child to go to camp?

How can your group together please God by using the resources he has given you? Consider the possibilities, pray, and take action.

Before the next meeting read chapter 8 in *Inverted*.

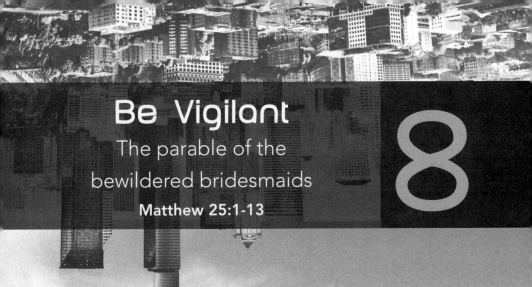

Be Vigilant
The parable of the bewildered bridesmaids
Matthew 25:1-13

8

The Bottom Line: This story is not about women who refused to share, it's about women who refused to prepare.

The Goal of This Session: To motivate us to be serious about being ready for Jesus' return. We will examine and discard inadequate understandings of the parable and learn that there is a limit to borrowing and sharing. We will recognize that waiting for Jesus' return is not a passive state of mind and we will evaluate our individual preparedness.

LEADER PREPARATION

Read Matthew 25:1-13.

Read chapter 8 in the book *Inverted* by Tom Ellsworth.

Pray for focus during your discussion. It is so tempting to digress to

"When will he return?" Ask God to help your group grasp that readiness is not about knowing when, but learning how to keep busy while waiting.

CONNECT
Bailout

When was the last time someone asked you to bail them out of an urgent situation? Maybe they wanted you to lend them a little cash for lunch? lend your car for a quick trip somewhere? babysit for their kids? What other kinds of "bailout" situations have you heard about or been part of? Share with the group.

How do you determine whether or not you will rescue the person in the above scenarios? Do you consider how the person could have prepared for the crisis?

Preparedness Quiz

Give yourself one point for each of these items that is applicable to you.

_____ I am sure that my current registration and insurance information for my car are in my glove box.

_____ I have a first-aid kit in my car.

_____ I know how to operate the jack in case I have to change a flat tire.

_____ I have jumper cables in my car.

_____ I keep an extra quart of oil in my trunk.

_____ I keep a gas can in my trunk.

_____ I have AAA or some other kind of roadside assistance plan.

_____ My family has practiced a fire drill from our home.

_____ My family has a code word in case someone needs to pick up my children from school.

Give a round of applause to the person or persons in your group who are most prepared for family emergencies and for safe travel on the highways.

STUDY

Read the parable aloud.

1. Jesus begins the parable with the words "at that time." What time? See Matthew 24:42, 44.

2. What do you see as the "job description" for the bridesmaids?

3. In what way were the wise bridesmaids prepared for a long night? What did the other bridesmaids fail to do that earned them the description "foolish"?

4. Why was it wise to refuse the request of the bridesmaids who didn't have any oil?

5. Read verse 11. When the foolish bridesmaids returned later, can you tell whether they had what they had earlier lacked? At that point, did it matter that they now had the oil?

6. Why were the foolish bridesmaids unable to get inside? What reason did the doorkeeper give for not admitting the latecomers?

7. Which of these could be Jesus' main application of his parable? Explain your answer.

   - It's time you all started sharing with each other.
   - If you loved me, you wouldn't fall asleep while waiting for me.
   - Don't agree to be in a wedding if you can't afford the cost.

- If you study the wedding invitation enough, you'll know exactly what time to show up.
- Don't be caught unprepared.
- Waiting for Jesus' return involves more than speculating about the time.

8. Read Luke 12:35-40. What similarities do these verses have with the parable in Matthew 25:1-13? What are the differences?

LEADER'S NOTES

Here is some helpful background information concerning this parable.

When: Jesus told this story just days before his triumphal entry into Jerusalem, the week before his death.

Who was in the audience: the disciples (see Matthew 24:1).

Why Jesus told this story: The disciples asked Jesus about the sign of his coming and the end of the age.

Other Gospels where this parable is recorded: none.

Other places where Jesus says, "Watch" or "Keep watch": Matthew 24:42; Luke 12:15-40.

Surprise! The word describing the *wise* bridesmaids is the same word translated as "shrewd" to describe the dishonest steward in the previous session, the parable of the street-smart steward. The word describing the *foolish* bridesmaids is related to our word *moron*, and also *sophomore*, which means "wise fool."

APPLY

9. The author of *Inverted* describes the foolish bridesmaids as "bewildered." What were they bewildered about? In your opinion, should they have been bewildered? Why or why not?

10. Read the Scriptures listed below. Then place the references in the correct column, according to how they relate to the headings.

Matthew 22:1-3
John 14:2, 3
1 Corinthians 2:9
Ephesians 2:10
2 Timothy 2:21
2 Timothy 4:2
Hebrews 11:16
1 Peter 1:13
1 Peter 3:15
Revelation 21:2

God has or is preparing something for us.	Believers are to prepare for _____ by _____ .

11. Give yourself one point for each of these items that characterizes you.

_____ I have a will.
_____ I have arranged for guardians for my children (if you have children under eighteen).

_____ I have a medical (living) will.

_____ I have made attempts to mend broken relationships.

_____ I have made attempts to talk about Jesus with people I care about.

_____ I have used my time and resources to the best of my ability.

_____ I am intentionally living my life to glorify God.

_____ I have periodic spiritual checkups to make sure I am staying on track as I live out God's calling for me.

How did you score? Heaping guilt on yourself for unfinished business is not appropriate or helpful. But choosing to be more intentional can create a different outcome. What stands out to you as an area where you need to focus your attention?

12. The bridesmaids fell asleep while waiting. Some people play games on their phone, call a friend, or read a book to pass the time while they wait. Waiting can make you crazy or waiting can make you strong. Read these verses and write down actions or attitudes to adopt while waiting for Jesus' return.

Mark 15:43

Luke 3:15

John 3:29

Romans 8:25

Jude 21

13. A. T. Robertson said, "Ignorance of the time of the second coming is not an excuse for neglect, but a reason for readiness" (*Word Pictures in the New Testament*, Vol. 1 [Nashville: Broadman, 1930], 198). What do you want to be doing when Jesus returns? What needs to change in order to fulfill that goal? Choose one area you want to focus on:

- changes in my growth plan
- changes in my attitudes
- changes in my prayer life
- changes in my activities
- changes in my boldness

INVERSION > GOING BEYOND DISCUSSION

The closing section in chapter eight of *Inverted* reminds us of how much Jesus treasures his bride, the church. How could your group take on a project that would enhance the beauty of your local congregation?

- Is there an area outside that needs sprucing up?
- Is there a classroom that needs a new coat of paint?
- What about something beyond the building? Could your group serve as greeters for several weeks, warmly welcoming people as they arrive?
- What about volunteering to be the hospitality team for an upcoming activity? You could be the set-up, serving, and clean-up team.
- Perhaps you could be the face of your church at a local soup kitchen. Sign up for a day to prepare and serve the dinner.

Find a way to enhance and beautify the reputation of Jesus' lovely bride.

Before the next meeting, review the themes and applications of *Inverted*. Be prepared to share how this study has impacted you. Which parable turned out to be your favorite? Which lesson are you still struggling with? Did your group carry out any of the suggested projects? How do those help you translate your faith into action? Your transparency has the potential to bring your group closer together. Bring one idea about the next possible study for your group.